The 3 Keys of Execution:

Simple Ideas. Extraordinary Results.

Kent Vaughn
David Williams

Praise for *The 3 Keys of Execution*

"Finally, a brilliant book that makes Execution simple, with practical wisdom so everyone can be fully engaged at every level."

Stephan Mardyks, Founder/CEO of Wisdom Destinations and coauthor of Quantum Negotiation

"Kent, David & Brian have distilled the essence of successful Execution with their 3 Keys and ABC's. I love the simplicity of their approach. You'll learn the formula of how to execute with speed and precision, but also equally important, when and why execution fails. If you've struggled with accomplishing team and company goals, you need this book."

David M.R. Covey, CEO of SMCOV and coauthor of the bestselling book, Trap Tales: Outsmarting the 7 Hidden Obstacles to Success.

A must read for all leadership, The 3 Keys of Execution, really lets us roll in the dough!

Peter D'Andrea, President 5-Star Pizza Inc dba Domino's Pizza (owns than 40 Dominos across the North America)

"Execution might seem easy and something obvious for all managers and executives. However, I have over the years discovered that almost every company that I have been involved in, have been struggling with execution. It often gets lost in complex methods or insurmountable amounts of daily tasks and unclear priorities. Therefore, I am delighted by how Kent, David and Brian have pinned execution down to the core of getting things done. The 3 Keys of Execution is a must read for every leader in business."

Johan Frilund, CEO

"I've tried execution approaches in the past and have been successful, but The 3 Keys nails it. Blaze has taken something which has been complicated and made it substantially simpler. Their approach to Execution turns the lights on in every room in the house and everyone can see what everyone is doing. No more hiding. Just awesome."

Danny Jones, Senior Executive, Hospitality

Perhaps the most profound statement in this book is on page 84, "Most people really do want to perform well! Many times, they don't because they don't know how to, or they're so busy doing "stuff" they never move to the next level. They need a great coach or director to help them." Isn't this the central problem in any business?

The 3 Keys of Execution articulates, though both concept and antidote, a simple and fundamental template for Problem Solving and Execution which will work for individuals and organizations. This is not a "How To" book, but details a flexible yet structured methodology which an organization can implement, grow and prosper. The EYIP application is a fine example of what software should be, one that supports the process and amplifies the intelligence of the users.

Paul Serex

Senior Lecturer, The Kelley School of Business, Indiana University

Having led execution for nearly 20 years, both in self and team settings, I have been exposed to many execution tools. Some are complex, outline systems that eventually become noise, or are hard to communicate and repeat.

This book communicates the universal truths of Execution, and offers a refreshing and modern application. This is a step by step instruction manual for effective and repeatable Execution. This is how all of us set ourselves apart from our future selves.

Jared Rice, Senior Operations Leader, National Landscaping Company

No doubt Execution processes have been around for quite some time but what the team at Blaze has done is to simplify what other groups make way too complicated. The emphasis they put on people engagement is the secret sauce sorely needed in today's business environment.

Arnie Roberts – Senior Executive with 30 years experience with the Fortune 500 in Global Supply Chain

"It is unfortunate we didn't have this Leadership Tool when we rolled out a well-known execution process across 3 plants, 1.2M square feet and 250 associates.

I've read the entire book and can easily relate to all the examples. They are real life events that EVERYONE deals with daily, weekly within their lives."

Gary Cunningham

Global Senior Operations Leader, Biopharmaceutical

The gentlemen of Blaze Performance Solutions offer a simplified, yet mature approach for getting things done in your organization - and in your personal life. By following the 3 Keys to Execution, you and your team will establish a culture of setting attainable and focused goals that lead to organizational growth.

Dr. Twyla Casey Wells

Johnston Community College, Smithfield, NC

'Having run Execution processes with other organizations in my career, I was pleasantly surprised with the how team at Blaze has greatly simplified the approach to Execution. The reason track athletes fail to break records is because they are racing for the finish line rather than racing through the finish line. Blaze is racing through the finish line with their Execution approach: Simplicity, Visibility and Accountability.'

Neil Carter, Senior Executive, National Landscaping Company

"I like it...Simplicity, Visibility and Accountability. 3 words and methods that we who have worn the uniform understand and appreciate it. However, no matter how much we know these basic principles, if we are honest with ourselves, we often forget to apply them."

Brigadier General Jason Bohm, USMC, Chief of Staff at STRIKFORNATO

Disclaimer: The recommendation listed above by General Jason Bohm is not an endorsement of, by or from the USMC or the DOD or shall be construed as such.   This is a personal recommendation only and shall be recognized only as a personal recommendation.

"During many years of consulting, teaching and leading in organizations, I have read countless books about managing and leading to success.   Most have one thing in common.   The author is as in love with his/her words as with his/her ideas.   These books are generally full of tedious explanations that result in what I call "the mid-book doldrums".   They complicate the simple and act as a great tool to remedy sleepless nights.   The ideas may be good, but they are often lost in the literary fluff.   Not this book!   The 3 Keys of Execution presents a potent dose of reality iced with basic common sense.   It's simple, easy to follow, and provides a welcome clarity not often found in management literature.   If your purpose is to lead an organization or yourself to success (and I can't imagine any other purpose), this book is for you.   This process will not only open the door to success but will lead you through.   Simple really is better!"

W. Wooldridge

Retired CHRO, Professor and Management Consultant

Table of Contents

Foreword

As I was picking up this book, I had a hundred excuses as to why I didn't have time to read it. I am a busy person. Seriously busy.

My travel schedule has been ridiculous. I have team members that "just need five minutes of my time." I have college kids who need their allowance. I have deadlines at work. I have messages to return. I am buried under 2000 emails in my unread box. Waa Waa Waa! And, then I took a pause and thought, *Hum why not? Maybe I will learn just one thing from these guys that will help bring closure to the chaos of my great big daunting Daily-To- Do List.* After all, I do know one of the authors, David, who is a thought-leader in the space of effectiveness and execution. I paid good money to watch him speak a few years back, and he made an impression on me.

Yet, somehow my work life and personal life have once again gotten out of control. Once again, I don't feel like I am accomplishing what I need to, on a daily, monthly and quarterly basis—let alone, fulfilling any my personal goals and dreams. So, out of desperation and curiosity, along with a healthy dose of skepticism, I picked up this little gem of a book, *3 Keys of Execution* and dove into it. It didn't take long before I started cracking up. Could the authors possible be talking about me or some of my team members in this book? Had someone snuck into our morning meeting and watched us flounder with the best of intentions? Ahhh, pretty sure yes. And why is that? Because hard-working folks pretty much suffer from the same crazy issues all over the workplace. How do we get stuff done? How do we get our teams motivated and behind their goals? Oh, and what *are* the goals for that matter? Why did I come into work and go to that meeting? What's the reason again? And what are we hoping to accomplish at the end of the day? Sound familiar? I'm guessing—yes. Laugh out loud. It's happening every minute in every company around the globe.

So, what happened after I read this book? Let's put it this way: Game Change. Seriously. *3 Keys of Execution* delivers "the secret antidote to the chaos of mediocrity." I will compare this read to one of my favorite business books, *Rework* by Jason Fried and David Heinemeier Hansson. I love *Rework* and always have several copies of it. Why? Because it's easy to read. It's simple. It's short and sweet and to the point. You can pick it up year after year and quickly go to the chapter that is relevant to you at that time.

3 Keys of Execution will not disappoint. It, too, is an easy read, but more importantly, it resonates as a portal for change to daily, weekly, and—yes—quarterly behavior. It seems to deliver an easy roadmap to achieving one's goals. *3 Keys of Execution* lays it out plain and simple.

In my past life, my teams practiced these easy steps and won awards, changed the trajectory our business, received promotions, accolades, bonuses, and freedom. My company was and is a coveted place to work, for its culture, integrity, and business acumen. When asked "How we do it?" I can now simply hand them this book.

Embrace some new knowledge and get your life back.

Cheers,

Angela Mitcham

Successful, Fun Loving, Hospitality and Finance Senior Executive

Acknowledgements

It is truly an amazing story that brought us, the 3 primary partners of Blaze Performance Solutions, together. While we each come from different career backgrounds—manufacturing, transportation and logistics, healthcare and consulting—the concept of execution has guided our careers to merge and brought us to the stark realization that most industries, most companies, struggle with effectively executing strategies to achieve their goals. A simple Google search will reveal that this is not due to a lack of "training," but rather the lack of an effective, formulaic approach to execution. That's where we come in. We, as pioneers in the micro -learning and gamification space, have created something we believe can positively impact the results your company can achieve.

What excites us about this book, and about our approach to execution, is that there are no excuses, no easy ways out, no way to cheat the system. You either do what needs to be done or you don't. There is nowhere to hide, no way to let accountability fade away. Perhaps that sounds harsh, but for most, it is refreshing. Execution builds teams and leads to the most revolutionary results for both companies and individuals. While we are excited to have you join us on this path, we want to be transparent and let you know crazy things will arise—life happens and showing up is no longer good enough. However, if you implement the techniques (in this book) AND utilize our mobile-enabled Tech tool (*Execution in Your Pocket®*), you will see results like you've never imagined. You will create a culture of effectiveness that will amaze you. Get ready, it will be an extraordinary journey!

Scan the QR code or type in the link to *The Execution In Your Pocket® website.*

https://blazeperformancesolutions.com/execution-in-your-pocket

Introduction

At the age of 11, Florence Chadwick won first place in a six-mile race across the choppy waters of the San Diego Bay Channel. This win sparked a 19-year-long career as a competitive swimmer. She went on to become the first woman to swim the English Channel both ways. On July 4, 1952, at the age of 34, Florence attempted to be the first woman to swim the 21 miles from Catalina Island to the California Coast of Palos Verde. The water was cold as ice and the fog so dense she could barely see her support boats as they watched vigilantly for sharks and signs of distress.

Unfortunately, the fog never lifted as she swam mile after mile, hour after hour. Her support crew fired rifles at the sharks as she kept swimming. Finally, after 15 hours and 55 minutes, the fog became so dense she did not know where she was. She dejectedly told her crew to pull her out of the water. Imagine her dismay when she learned she was less than a mile from shore. With her skills and stamina, she most assuredly could have swum that last mile. Later that day, Florence told a reporter, "Look, I'm not excusing myself, but if I could have seen land, I know I could have made it."

Part of the magic formula for achieving any goal is keeping it in front of you. What's the probability for success if the goal gets lost in the shuffle of everything else we have going on? How many times has this happened to you and your organization? You begin the year, or the quarter, or the project, with the very best intentions—then life happens. You lose sight of your goal and failure follows.

With a plan, a process and our Execution in Your Pocket® (EIYP) tool, it is possible to break this pattern of failure and achieve the success you've always dreamt of. In this book, we will share with you the hard-earned skills and experience we've acquired over fifty plus years of devoting ourselves and our companies to the discipline of execution.

The Formula for Execution

At the beginning of each year, or quarter, we plan, we dream, and we put together strategies to be as successful as possible. We confidently proclaim that "This time it will be DIFFERENT." We decide we WON'T get caught up in "all the little stuff." We won't get off track. We won't lose focus. However, the day-to-day tasks of life and business have a way of getting in the way of our most important goals. This is something that happens to most of us; we head off trying to fight the good fight, but we do so unarmed. It is unacceptable to allow all the distractions and competing priorities get in the way of achieving greater success. What we must understand is that there is a formula for execution—simplicity, visibility, accountability. This formula is all you need on your path to executing strategies to achieve your goals.

You will want to complicate it. You will want to add more to your plate. But every time you add more, you create an environment for the "Diffusion of Responsibility." You allow yourself to say "Well, I had to do…" or "There's not enough time to do…" The truth is that there is never enough time to do everything, so you MUST follow the formula of Simplicity, Visibility and Accountability to reach your goals. This will give you the armor you need to ward off all the other distractions, eliminate the diffusion of responsibility, and give you the ability to succeed at even the most intimidating goals.

There will be times when you may want to skip one of the *Keys* because you "don't have time." This mentality will lead to failure. We have seen it time and time again; people give themselves the excuse that "other things came up" or they were "busy with another priority." When teams allow this thinking, it becomes a pattern. The teams then struggle for years without really progressing on their most important goals. The good news is that if you follow this formula, you will achieve goals you never knew possible, grow an effective culture, and deliver the best work of your career.

Understanding the Ecosystem of the 3 Keys

Many companies, and more personally, you as a leader, executive, or frontline employee will need to make sense of the *3 Keys of Execution* and apply these lessons in a frenetic changing environment to remain competitive and relevant. Leaders must bring into focus those things that broaden, increase, or even reinvent the advantage to the organization. You must recognize and understand what is important in your company.

Conventional wisdom argues that the core of operating a business is heavily focused on the basics of strategy, goals, customers, systems, processes, and value statements to increase market share in a vigorous competitive market. A comprehensive study of most companies shows a disproportionate amount of focus is centered on how to get goods and services to the market. This emphasis on strategy is universally accepted, yet the ultimate competitive advantage is execution. This one elusive idea may seem fairly basic and yet is universally underestimated in its difficulty and importance.

Consider for a moment this simple question: What do Ritz Carlton and Motel 6 have in common? Or Nordstrom and Wal-Mart? The first response may be they are hoteliers or retailers in very different segments of their markets. The answer? They are all successful in their industry and defined market! All four of these companies have similar strategic initiatives and processes to deliver results. Ritz Carlton and Motel 6 have built strong brands selling a customer a clean room with the expected amenities. Nordstrom and Wal-Mart both offer retail products and a particular customer experience. Furthermore, they have identified their most important goals and are actively providing extraordinary service in their respective markets. Each of these companies follows a proven pattern or strategy for success. The broader question that must be answered is this: Why are these companies at the top of their industries?

Many businesses look much the same in their core operations but deliver very different results. If you examine any market segment you will see there are organizations at the top of the industry and those limping along to survive while practicing the same core techniques. Nordstrom and Wal-Mart are among the best performers because they consistently execute their strategies from the C-Suite to the front line.

Ritz Carlton and Motel 6 have done the same thing in their industries. They've identified the goals for every leader and employee, who, in turn, have identified their ABCs for success—Activities, Behaviors and Commitment. Perhaps even more importantly, they've found a way to get everyone from the C-Suite to the front line to consistently execute these every day.

In contrast, look no further than JC Penney to see an organizational structure in disarray because it doesn't consistently perform the activities and exhibit the behaviors required to achieve a competitive advantage in its market. The company's performance has been so poor that the board recently fired a struggling CEO and brought back the previous CEO, who has since been fired as well. All because it failed to focus on two essential groups: customers and employees! As a matter of fact, a recent marketing campaign focused on thanking customers for returning and forgiving JC Penny.

Eating Last and Servant Leadership

Another important distinction for many of the best organizations is great leadership. One of our basic tenets at Blaze Performance Solutions is that everyone is a leader. As a leader, ask yourself this question, "Am I eating last?"

In the Marine Corps—and most of the armed services— non-commissioned officers eat last day in and day out. And the officers they report to eat last. Are you "eating last" from a leadership perspective within your organization? Are you making sure that you are leading your team members effectively and living by the example of the United States Marines? Now you might be thinking "Wait a minute. I'm not in the military." Even still, ask yourself this question, *Am I figuratively, spiritually, emotionally eating last?*

Execution is a system that needs leadership.

To be clear, we're not talking about ensuring that everyone goes in the line before you at the company Christmas party. What we are really talking about is the concept of serving. Are you really serving those on your team?

You see, as a true servant leader, you need to understand this concept of eating last. True servant leadership brings about dynamic results when it comes to execution. What are you doing as a leader to help your team members win the game? What are you doing as a leader to help your team members cross the finish line?

Recruits in boot camp at Parris Island, South Carolina, have it drilled into them—you do not leave a fellow Marine behind—no matter what. If they are struggling, you help them, you teach them, you motivate them, but you do not leave them behind. Marines rely on fellow Marines to help in strength building, encouragement, and motivation. Every leader in the Marine Corps is born out of this team mentality.

What happens if you implement that same concept within your own organization? What happens if you say, "We are not going to leave anybody behind. We're going to help everyone cross the finish line!"?

It will begin to change the way you lead your whole team, the way you lead your entire organization. *The 3 Keys of Execution* are not just about winning the game it is about HOW you win the game.

Simplicity, visibility and accountability—these 3 things work best when combined with a servant leadership mindset. Ask yourself, *What am I doing that shows my team I'm here to serve them and to help them meet our goals?*

What are you doing as a leader to make sure that they are going to be able to win the game? How are you meeting the needs of your team? Are you eating last within your own organization? If not, then that might be the problem.

Introduction of The 3 Keys of Execution

Because you've picked up this book, we know you at least hope to find a way to be better than last year. That's an important start! For now, we want you to focus just on starting; throughout this book, we'll show you how to finish. Yes, there will be some hard parts, and we will help you through those as well. Mile 18 of the marathon is coming, the mile when most of us hit the wall and want to stop, but with some preparation and a time proven process we will show you how to be successful.

This morning I was listening to Les Brown who quoted Charles Swindoll when he said, "An Optimist sees an opportunity in every calamity, a Pessimist sees a calamity in every opportunity." In this book, we will not try to convince you to become more of an optimist per se, but we will give you some tools which will help you find success no matter where you are or where you've been.

Have you ever known someone who seems to have the "Midas Touch"? Everything seems to go their way, everything they touch turns to gold. Many people might say something like "That person is so lucky!" Have you ever felt that way about someone else?

Luck is such an interesting word. There is a saying in the South that goes something like this, "Even a blind hog can find an acorn every once in a while." All of us have been lucky at least once in our lives, but the goal is to consistently and intentionally achieve success in every area of our lives. Let me assure you that success in life is not based on genetics, upbringing, geography or anything else. Of course, there are people who started out with more than you. But it isn't about where you start; it's where you're going and, ultimately, where you finish. Whether you have ten talents, or one, you can either squander them or develop them.

I've devoted the majority of the last thirty years helping people achieve more of what they want to achieve and become who they want to become. My partners, David Williams and Brian Cox, have been equally immersed in this kind of work for decades.

We know that ultimate success does not boil down to optimism, pessimism or even luck. Sure, those things may have an impact, but we know the real secret to success is achieved by following a repeatable process with which you will create and follow a road map for your own success. We have done this with organizations with ten employees and with 10s of 1000s of employees and with people just like you who want to get better. The real key for everyone is always the same, not just creating the plan but consistently executing the ABCs (the Actions, Behaviors and Commitments) required to accomplish their goals.

Let me share a simple example. Let's imagine that one night, at about 9:30, you're a little hungry. You go into the kitchen and grab a handful of peanuts. By the way, that handful of about 35 peanuts, is a serving of 170 calories. After eating the peanuts you're no longer hungry and you go to bed. Sure, just one night eating an extra 170 calories is no big deal. But what if you were to start eating that handful of peanuts every night? For most people, in just 21 days of consistently eating an extra 170 calories, they will gain about a pound. If you do this for the entire year, that means the average person will gain around 17 pounds, all from just 35 extra peanuts every night before bedtime. Sure, there are plenty of other factors to consider when it comes to your health and weight. But the fact remains that consistently adding extra caloric intake will make just about anyone gain weight!

Let's turn this example around. What if you were to cut back each night the equivalent of that handful of peanuts? In 21 days, you would lose one pound. In a year, you would lose 17, all with just a small change in behavior.

Now the fact is, with extreme measures, you could lose 20 pounds this week. Undoubtedly, the benefit would not be worth the cost. So often, people believe it requires massive changes in their lives to see improved results. The problem with massive change is that, in most cases, it is unsustainable. In this book we will give you a process for making small, consistent changes that equate to massive results over time. We will focus on the ABC's (Actions, Behavior and Commitments) you need to achieve your goals.

In the last chapter of the book we will also introduce you to our Dynamic, Gamified Platform for success called *Execution in Your Pocket*®. It's a tool you can access from your phone (or any web enabled device) to help you stay focused every day on the ABC's and your goals.

As I close this introduction, I'm reminded of something Willis Whitney said, "People often have 1,000 reasons why they cannot do something, when all they really need is one reason why they can." So, what is your reason why? Here is something I know about you already: you deserve success and happiness in life. Your family deserves it. It doesn't matter if you're the grandson of sharecroppers, like me, or were born with a silver spoon; you were made to succeed, to make a difference, to achieve! Welcome to a new level of success in your life and in your career!

We've created a very easy to understand, 3-step process to dramatically increase your personal and organizational execution. We call it the *3 Keys of Execution*. Those *3 Keys* are Simplicity, Visibility and Accountability. Here's how we define each of those terms:

Simplicity – Everyone knows exactly what the goals are, understands the job to be done and understands who owns each piece of those goals.

Visibility – Everyone can see all the daily and weekly Activities and Behaviors accomplished by each team member.

Accountability – Everyone accounts daily and weekly for their performance of the Activities and Behaviors they Committed to doing.

Take a minute and think about any goal you've ever achieved. As you consider that success, you will find that you utilized all 3 of these Keys, in one form or another, to achieve it.

One of my personal goals has been to run a marathon. One day, my running partner came to me with a plan to run a marathon about 10 months in the future. At that point in time we were typically running 3 or 4 times a week and each run was about 3 or 4 miles long. Now my partner, Mike Gibson is a *real* runner. In fact, he ran cross country in high school and in college. I, on the other hand, am a guy who happens to run—and there is a huge difference. On this day in July, Mike was trying to turn my personal goal into reality. Without even realizing it, Mike followed the *3 Keys of Execution*. Here's how:

Simplicity – We set a goal to complete the Music City Marathon on April 26th of the next year. Complete all the scheduled practice runs along the way.

Visibility – We created a running schedule utilizing the plan of a well-known running coach who had helped 1000s of people run marathons and other distance races.

Accountability – There was no hiding from this one. We each had to show up for every scheduled run as planned.

Here's what's interesting to note, over the next 10 months, in spite of business travel, vacations and other life events.

Notwithstanding rain, snow, the flu and even a torn meniscus, neither of us ever missed a scheduled run. Along the way, we ran a 5k, an 11-mile Thanksgiving run in the Smoky Mountains—through rain so heavy they closed the park—and our first half marathon to boot.

Two weeks prior to the marathon, Mike tore his meniscus in one of his knees and had a surgeon tell him to cancel the race. We were heartbroken! Thankfully a surgeon friend of ours, Dr. Paul Becker, said that the damage was done and running the marathon would not make it any worse.

Because of all that work and preparation, we ran that Marathon in Nashville, Tennessee in April of the following year. We started slowly to protect Mike's knee and after many opportunities for failure we crossed the finish line within seven minutes of our goal time. Now, that is nothing particularly glorious. Literally millions of people run marathons every single year. But here's the kicker, how many more millions of people *say* they want to run a marathon but never follow through? The *3 Keys* is a process you can use to achieve any goal you really set your mind to.

Sound too simple to work? That is exactly why the process does work, because it is simple. It is easy to remember and apply. There are so many things coming at you every day but that is no excuse for not accomplishing the most important goals in your life. The goals you really want and need to maniacally focus on!

How many times have you gotten to the end of a year being surprised by two facts:

1. How quickly the year has gone!

2. How little progress you made on your goals and aspirations!

How many years do you have to waste like that? Isn't this the year that you need to pick out just one goal for work and one for your personal life that you are going to crush? Some people describe this as living life to the fullest or with no regrets or in Crescendo!

On my desk, I have this reminder posted, "Live life in Crescendo, Increase in Force and Intensity."

What if you and everyone on your team started thinking and acting this way? What if every one of you started focusing on one or two Actions (A's) you could take and Behaviors (B's) you could exhibit every day to live life to the fullest? Think of the combined power and impact of this kind of planned and orchestrated behavior. With this kind of consistent effort, success is all but assured!

Why Execution Fails

Short answer? Too. Many. Goals.

There is a tendency to have way too many goals. Years ago, I started working with the COO of a large logistics company who said he had 5 top goals his people had to Execute more consistently. I asked him how long they had been working on the goals and how they were doing on them. He said they had been working on these 5 goals for over 3 years and were making progress on one of them.

I said to him, "You're telling me that in more than 3 years you have only made real progress on just one of your top 5 goals?" After he sheepishly agreed, I suggested he try something different this year. I asked him, "How about if you pick just one of those goals and get the entire organization maniacally focused on that one goal?"

To which he immediately retorted, "But I need all 5 of the goals!"

I almost laughed as I replied, "Of course you *want* all 5, but if you keep doing the same thing you've been doing, how much are you likely to achieve this year?"

Many people face this exact same dilemma. There are lots of things they want to achieve and therefore they spread themselves thin, making slight progress on each task, but never make any real progress toward their most important goal.

In Dave Ramsey's debt reduction program, he offers a suggestion for paying off multiple credit cards. He recommends focusing on paying off the card with the smallest balance. Make the minimum payments on the rest of the cards, while making double, or even triple, the minimum payment on that card with the smallest balance. Once you have paid off that card, go on to the next one and do the same thing. He calls this "The Debt Snowball Effect," because as you pay extra money on just one card you quickly get it paid off and can focus on the next one, then the next one, and so on. With this approach you'd be surprised how, in just a year or two, you can pay off all your credit card debt. Compare that to paying the minimum payment on each credit card. Have you ever looked at the statement which tells you how long it will take to pay off the credit card if you just pay the minimum? It can often take twenty years or more to pay off the debt. Isn't that crazy?

This is exactly what happens with our goals. If we have too many of them and spend the minimum amount of time on each one, it may take us decades to ever improve. Or, even worse, we ultimately give up and stop trying.

Even when you are working on a goal that is extremely important to you, it's so easy to lose focus. That is why we must remind ourselves of the importance of that goal daily and stay focused on completing the ABCs to accomplish it.

Why Excitement Wears Off

We've all experienced the excitement of setting a goal and imagining ourselves achieving it. Have you ever imagined scoring the winning points in the championship game, spelling the word correctly in the spelling bee, or closing the multi-million-dollar deal or project for your company? Of course, you have. We have all set many, many wonderful goals in our minds. It is human nature to believe we can achieve more. Although life and circumstances can beat this innate belief out of us, I believe that every child is born with the belief that they can achieve important things in their lives.

A friend of mine tells the story of a Chief Nursing Officer at a large Atlanta hospital who confessed, "When we hire young nurses right out of college, they want to change the world. They want to help and heal people. They want to make a difference. Unfortunately, it only takes us about 3 years to beat this out of them."

I heard the same story from the Assistant Principal of the inner-city Elementary School my daughter taught at in Phoenix, Arizona. She said "These young teachers really want to make a difference and it is nearly impossible to keep them for more than two or 3 years. The work is so hard and the circumstances of the children so difficult."

So why does the excitement wear off? There are many reasons. Nursing and Teaching have some very specific difficulties in their fields, as do many other fields, but for many of the organizations we've worked with over the last twenty years here are some of issues that are real excitement killers:

1. They don't understand why.

The surest way to eradicate excitement is to have people chasing after a goal or activity and they don't understand the value of what they're doing. The way to overcome this issue is to ensure that everyone understands *why* you are setting this goal and what value it will create. For example: Achieving this goal will allow us to serve more people in our community. Or, improving customer service will help us retain customers, grow our revenue and hire more employees. An essential part of getting buy-in and maintaining excitement is that everyone really understands why this goal is important to the organization and what it will ultimately do for them. We need to tell people how the goal will benefit them, your customers/patients or students.

2. They're too busy.

In every organization we see fewer people doing more work. Unfortunately, that is just a fact of life and is not likely to change. But, if I don't see the value of the goal and I'm already working as hard as I can, it's not likely the new goal is going to get a lot of consistent attention.

3. The Blame Game.

So often departments and people spend a lot of time pointing fingers at each other, or their difficult circumstances, to compensate for their lack of success at achieving their goals. Compare this to one of my first Execution Clients who got so good at achieving their goals that they started to walk with a bit of a swagger because of their new-found success. In fact, they said to their senior leader: "give us any goal, any challenge and we'll get it done." That kind of excitement and confidence is contagious. Have you ever seen the football team that holds up four fingers when the fourth quarter starts? In essence they're saying, "We've been here before, we know what to do, we own the 4th quarter, we will win!"

4. No ABCs.

There are always more than enough things for people to do in a day. The ABCs are the daily Actions and Behaviors and the weekly Commitments each person needs to do to achieve their goals. When you break goals down to these daily and weekly behaviors and then hold each other accountable for completing them, your success is almost guaranteed.

5. Are we Winning or Losing?

Think about how exciting it is to know you are winning at something. Life and work are tough, and it can be easy to feel like we're not making progress each day or week. This is why it is essential to have a way for people to be able to identify daily that they're making progress. Think about the engagement and power that comes from each person knowing that every single day, no matter what else happens, they've at least accomplished one or two actions and behaviors that are moving them, their team and the organization positively forward on their goals! When people are part of a winning team, they're not likely to give up and leave, or worse, give up and stay!

6. They are left to figure it out on their own.

Giving people freedom to innovate and do their jobs is great, but all too often leaders make an assignment and then leave people to figure things out on their own. Imagine the director of a play or musical or the coach of any sports team. After opening night, or the first game, what will that director or coach be doing? They will be working with the cast or team to review what went well and identify opportunities to get better.

They will do this after every performance or game. They couldn't imagine letting them perform for several weeks with no guidance, support or coaching. Isn't it odd this is exactly what happens in so many organizations? We leave people on their own with very little feedback until things go wrong or until the end of the quarter or year. The best organizations are continually striving to improve and are helping everyone consistently work together to identify ways to get better. Work is not usually an individual sport. Yes, there are plenty of jobs done by individual contributors, but it is usually a cast of people that deliver the results!

Since watching the show *Kung Fu* at 14, I have always wanted to earn a black belt in martial arts. For years I talked about it but never actually did anything about it. Isn't it that way with so many things in our lives? We say we want to do something but never actually get around to doing anything about it. Finally, at the age of 36, purely by accident, I met a Korean Master that so impressed me that I decided to finally stop dreaming and do something about that goal. For the next 3 years, I really focused on earning that black belt, attending classes, taking tests and practicing, all while traveling every week for my job. About six months before I was going to test for my First-Degree Black Belt, a friend of mine called me and asked if

I would run a marathon to earn money for cancer survivors. It was for a worthy cause, so I quickly agreed to run.

Almost instantly I started thinking about my travel schedule and how hard it had been to fit in all my Tae Kwon Do classes and practice for the last 3 years. How was I ever going to add in some extended running to prepare for a marathon? Now think about how often this has happened to you in your personal or professional life. You're working on an important goal and something else comes along that looks important as well. If you're not focused on a goal that is important to you, you could easily be distracted and start making the minimum payments on a laundry list of goals. That is no way to achieve success. By the way, within a couple of days I called my friend and told him I was within six months of earning my black belt and would have to take a rain check on running that marathon. I had to choose between making minimum payments or focusing to finish my first goal. What do I have to show for that decision? I have a black belt in Tae Kwon Do.

We're not saying you cannot achieve many goals in your life. What we are saying is you'll have a lot more consistent success if you identify just one or two that you're going to maniacally focus on this year. When you do that you've got a real shot at success.

Execute Like a Chess Champion

One of the critical components of leadership is the ability to envision. The ability to see beyond what is happening right here and now and to see ahead in the future. Good chess players can see five or six moves ahead before they move a single chess piece. The best chess players are not just thinking about their moves they are also considering their opponents next moves. We call this the ability to envision.

Are you looking ahead on your organization's chess board and asking, 'If we continue to execute these plays with excellence day in and day out, are we going to win the game, is it going to be enough to cross over the finish line?"

Leaders must have the ability to envision. They need to think beyond what's happening right here and now.

Are you making the right movements on the chess board? Are your moves, ABCs if you will (your activities, behaviors and commitments) going to help you cross the finish line and win the game?

Here is another example of envisioning: In late 2001, David was working for a large electronic manufacturer with over 200,000 employees worldwide and an excess of $21B in revenue. They made cell phones, copiers, printers, components for cell phone towers, printed circuit boards and computers. You name it, they made it. This was during the time the Motorola StarTAC, was the first really "cool" flip phone. It was the hottest phone on the market; when you flipped it open, it made you feel like a character on Star Trek.

David will never forget when a startup electronics company came to his organization to present a radical idea to his team. They proposed the idea that people would be able to watch television on their phone. They had a vision, a chess play if you will, that was looking five, six, seven plays into the future.

Keep in mind, the displays on all phones at that time were just one color. They either had a yellow, orange or a silver backlit screen with a black LCD readout; and this company has this vision of people watching television on their phones. WHAT!?

About 75% of the people in the room were thinking *This will never happen,* and 25% (David included) were thinking *Wow, this is pretty awesome!* Then the questions began. Will it be live TV? Just playback video? What would – what could –it be? What an example of the ability to envision.

This organization was thinking 2, 3, 5, even 10 years ahead of the game. As we all know, people all around the world are watching live video on their phones today.

When you think about leadership within your organization and the *3 Keys of Execution*, one of the most critical pieces, is to continually be looking at least two or 3 moves ahead of what is currently known; and ask if your current ABCs are going to help you win the game? If you do these things, consistently, are they going to get you the results you want?

When David was the plant manager of a large manufacturing plant in Tarboro, North Carolina, he and his team became excellent at the ability to see beyond what was currently known, and deeply understanding their ABCs. When the President would call to ask where his numbers would be at the end of the month, the team in Tarboro had done such a great job identifying the best activities and behaviors, that they could predict their financial performance within 2%. The Tarboro team not only knew they were going to win the game, they knew by *how much* they were going to win the game. They had the ability to be able to tell the president and CEO the final monthly score before the month was even halfway done! The team in Tarboro had visionary leadership. They could see beyond just one move on the chessboard. Why, because they had identified the ABCs which would allow them to successfully run their business.

Do you have the ability to envision? Can you look at the chessboard and predict where you're going to be in 5, 6, 7, 8 moves? Or are you only playing one move at a time? As every accomplished chess player will tell you, if you're only planning one move at a time, you will lose the game.

The Science of Simplicity

Is there really such a thing as the science of simplicity? George Whitesides says there is. He is an advocate for the minimalist approach when it comes to executive wardrobes. He encourages people to have a minimal amount of clothes in their wardrobes and make sure each piece of clothing they have is interchangeable with each other. By adopting this approach, the leader is able to focus on both the business as well as the personal. Who really wants to struggle on a daily basis with what to wear? Aren't there more important things to do in life? The answer is yes.

There are gurus in the interior design space who talk about the need of decluttering one's house. Currently, in the US, the self-storage industry is a $38 billion a year industry. There are more than 52,000 self-storage facilities in the USA with more than 2.3 billion square feet of rentable space. This volume of stuff could fill the Hoover Dam nearly 30 times. What's even more astonishing—it is primarily a US industry. We, as US citizens have so much stuff, we have created a whole new industry!

Let's stop, pause and think about this. We have successful thought leaders proclaiming the benefits of minimizing our wardrobes. We have successful thought leaders urging us to declutter our homes. If our personal lives need simplification and decluttering, there is a good chance our professional lives do too. We need to "declutter" our priorities and simplify the number of goals.

Simplicity

In the early 2000s I heard Jim Collins (author of several books including *Good to Great*) speak at a conference in Atlanta. In that speech, he said, "There is no breakout of Execution in America?" He elaborated that the 1990s were arguably the most profitable decade in the history of the United States and yet only about 25% of the companies who made significant amounts of money actually met their stated financial objectives. That is absolutely astounding! Anyone who has been around for a few decades knows that the economy is cyclical and that those times of financial success are going to eventually end, just as they did when the tech bubble burst in the late 1990s. The real problem is if people and organizations don't figure out the pattern for success when times are good, how will they ever do it when times are tough?

How and why do people and organizations quit before they finish? Before they cross the proverbial finish line? One reason is that people and organizations often don't stick with anything long enough to make any real progress on it. I think when it comes to goals, we all have a little ADD (Attention Deficit Disorder). We're always looking for the next silver bullet to improve our lives, our relationships, our health and yes, our business. We're a little like the dog that is constantly chasing after the next squirrel making lots of noise and expending lots of energy but never really catching anything.

Simplicity is the opposite of this. It is finally deciding what we're going to be great at doing. Malcom Gladwell researched studies which claim it takes about 10,000 hours of focused practice to become an expert at something. I'm not saying that you need to become an expert at anything. But, achieving your goals begins with getting serious about identifying the one goal you're going to devote the most energy on this year (maybe one for work and one for your personal life). I know you have lots of things you have to accomplish this year, but what is the one thing you're going to absolutely excel at by year end? So where do you start? What do you have to do? It all begins with getting clear about what the goal means to you, why you're doing it and what needs to be done to achieve it. If you have multiple people working on the same goal that presents a whole different set of challenges.

Have you ever played the telephone game? Here's how it goes. Gather 7 or 8 people and ask them to stand or sit in a circle. Whisper to the person on your left some fact like, "My family moved 17 times when I was growing up." Then ask that person to whisper this fact into the ear of the person standing or sitting to their left. Have each person do the same thing until the person to your right whispers the little fact into your ear. If you've ever played this game, you know what comes next. The fact whispered into your ear (after it has gone around the circle) is virtually unrecognizable from the fact you started with.

In any organization with more than one person this is exactly what happens to your goals. Once they get repeated a few times they become something very different than what you began with. When that happens, the likelihood of achieving those goals diminishes significantly. If that happens often enough, people finally just give up on success.

Several years ago, my wife and I dropped our daughter off at college almost 2,000 miles away from home. None of her old friends would be attending that University and she was more than a little concerned about being that far away from home and about how well she would do in college. Because of her hard work in high school she had earned a 25% scholarship (which we were all proud of) but she still had something to prove to herself.

As we walked around the campus one day I said to my daughter, "Elyse, I know you want to excel in school and ultimately graduate and get a good job. Hopefully that's the goal of everyone on this campus. I'm going to let you in on a little secret. It boils down to just 3 things. If you will focus on these 3 things, I promise you that you will excel. Would you like to know what those 3 things are?" I then shared with her 3 specific ABC's built on the *3 Keys* of Execution we are now sharing with you—simplicity, visibility, and accountability.

Over the next few weeks and months, I routinely asked my daughter how she was doing with those 3 things. She almost always said she was doing great on the first couple of things and trying to do well on the third one. I always tried to tell her how proud and grateful I was for her hard work, and that it would pay off. I had consistently asked her how she was doing because I knew that these 3 things really would help her be successful and I wanted her to be successful just as much as she did.

I'm delighted to report that in her first semester she got a perfect 4.0 on a 4.0 grading scale and in the next semester she got a 3.97. Those grades were good enough to get her 25% scholarship increased to a 100% scholarship. I'm not sure who was more excited about this, her or me! Elyse was so proud of herself, and she had every right to be. In her first year of college she truly excelled, which is often not the case for college freshman. They're miles away from home, on their own for the first time, and completely forget about their most important goals, why they're there, and what is most important to them.

This scenario is played out again and again across college campuses around the world. It happens just as much to people in the workplace.

There are so many distractions it is easy to lose sight of what's most important.

The great thing about figuring out how to excel at something is that we all want to share it with someone else. Two years after dropping Elyse off at college we took our son, Kimball, to the same University. One day as we were walking around and Elyse was excitedly showing off the campus, apparently Kimball expressed some concern about doing well. Elyse immediately responded: "Kimball it's only 3 things. If you stay focused on those *3 Keys,* you will do great. Don't worry I will help you." I must admit I was blown away. Not only had she internalized those *3 Keys,* but she was going to help your younger brother apply them and excel as well. She had always been the protective big sister, but she was taking it to a whole new level. I am proud to say that in Kimball's first year of college he got better grades than he had ever gotten in high school. Thanks to his hard work, his sister, and the *3 Keys!*!

Master of One vs. Jack of all Trades

Have you ever tried to be everything to everyone? How did it work out for you? We have asked this question hundreds, if not thousands of times during sessions with clients and inevitably the answer is the same—not well. We see it in many facets of life, personal and professional, but the easiest example is the personal side. If you always try to be there for everyone in your life, you run yourself ragged trying to be great, but eventually one of two things will happen:

1. You become mediocre or superficial in many relationships, or
2. You burn out because you took no time for yourself

Either of these outcomes will leave you worse for the wear, but you can avoid these outcomes by focusing on what is most important. In the professional world, we see the same thing happen. Leaders and team members never say no, so they divide their time between ALL THE THINGS and wind up struggling to or even failing to achieve their greatest goals. If ever there was a time where it was absolutely necessary to be a singular focused leader, it is when you have a HUGE goal to achieve.

That leaves us with a question to answer, how can you say no? It's a difficult question to answer, but the best way is to utilize logical propositions. Is this task, project, etc. going to help you meet your goal? If not, then no is the only answer. If it will help you meet your goal, then you need to find out if you are the right person to handle the task, if not, then you need to get the right person on the task immediately. Perhaps the answer is not "no", but instead "we need to get the right people involved". Then you must make sure everyone understands the importance of the activity, ensure it is able to be simply tied to the goal, make it visible to everyone and put an accountability system in place.

Simplicity: Remaining Relevant

Whenever I think of remaining relevant, I'm reminded of several examples, the first is an experience I had during my first week of business school back in the 1985. It was Economics class, and the Professor showed a picture of the Fortune 100 companies in America. I remember looking at the list and the only company I recognized was Wrigley. After a few moments the Professor said: "Many of you are looking rather quizzically at the list and there is good reason for that. You would not recognize most of the companies on the list because most of them are no longer in business. This is a list of the Fortune 100 companies in 1900. Today, only seven of those companies are still in business." You could have heard pin drop in the room. Who would have ever imagined that 85 years later most of those giant organizations would no longer be in business?

The professor went on to say that no company, no organization had a *right* to exist. The reason companies or any organization stay in business is because they provide value that people will pay for or want to support in some form or fashion. Think about the number of companies that used to be around, that no longer exist today. What happened to them? Why did they go out of business? There are as many reasons as there are failed companies; but many times, we find that these obsolete companies suffered from the same issue. They stopped being relevant. They stopped offering the goods and services people wanted or in the way they wanted them.

A year later at that same business school another professor told us about his great grandfather who in the early 1900s was the number one buggy whip manufacturer in America. He was a renowned leather goods maker in Virginia and people from all over the country purchased his items for their horse and buggies.

One day a young man from Detroit visited the leather manufacturing facility to see if he could get the company to make leather covers for the seats in his new horseless carriage (automobile). The business owner (my professor's great grandfather) said to the young man: "Son, we have been riding horses since the dawn of time. Your horseless carriage will never amount to anything. I have no interest in committing my manufacturing resources to a project which will surely fail." The young man, Henry Ford, went home to Detroit and found someone else to provide the leather for the seats in what became the Model T automobile.

Could this happen to your organization? Is there enough vision for the future? Is there a desire and a drive to remain relevant in a constantly evolving marketplace? It is imperative to focus on your current goals, but you must also ensure you are open to trying new things and pushing the limits.

Let's take a minute to review another company that lost its relevance. There are probably people reading this book that will not remember walking into a Blockbuster Video, but let me tell you, they were a HUGE company that wasted away to nothing, seemingly overnight. In 1994, Wayne Huizenga sold Blockbuster Video to Viacom for $8.4 Billion and for several years Blockbuster continued to flourish as they continued to focus on building more brick and mortar video rental stores. In fact, in 1989 there were 9,000 stores; one opened every 17 hours!

Here is a little-known fact, a large portion of their annual revenue came from charging their customer's late fees and rewind fees. I still remember the stickers, "Please Be Kind, Rewind," urging you to rewind the tape before returning it to the store). In 1997, a guy named Reed Hastings got charged a $40 late fee for not returning the movie *Apollo 13* on time. As you can imagine, he was incensed. He could have bought the movie for half that price! Mr. Hastings was so frustrated that he decided he had to figure out a better way to rent movies. He started a little company named Netflix (you may have heard of that company). As with any startup, this one was expensive to launch and even 3 years later after they launched, they were still not making a lot of money. They were focused on the business of home DVD subscriptions which was starting to get a pretty good following.

Now here's where it gets interesting. In 2000, Blockbuster was starting to lose money and started offering their own version of DVD delivery hoping to regain profitability. It was in this same year that Reed Hastings flew from his home in California to present an idea to the Blockbuster Executive team. His plan was very simple; he had already perfected the DVD delivery business so he proposed Blockbuster purchase Netflix for a mere $50 Million and he would run the Blockbuster delivery program under their name. As you can imagine, the Blockbuster Executives laughed Reed out of their offices, how dare him make such an offer to mighty Blockbuster? They would trounce Netflix at their own game.

Isn't it interesting how often people think that just because they know one business that they can figure out any other business, even if they are late to the party? When Wal-Mart decided to enter the grocery business, they had the good sense to buy the logistics company which had been supporting Kroger for years. The Korean car manufacturers Kia and Hyundai hired away the lead designers from Bentley and Audi in order to make their cars more attractive and reliable. Now that's one way to get a leg up on the competition, buy their inner most secrets.

As of 2019, there is only one Blockbuster store left which is located in Bend, Oregon. One store left out of over 9,000. Oh, and by the way, the market cap (valuation) of Netflix is now over $175 Billion. I bet Reed Hastings is incredibly grateful Blockbuster did not accept his offer to sell for $50 Million back in 2000. I'm not sure what kind of return that would be, but it is little like winning the lottery 1,000 times!

As a leader of an organization, a team or just yourself, don't be a Blockbuster. You want to be Netflix, Hyundai and Kia, shaping the market and giving value.

Consider this quote from futurist Alvin Toffler: "The illiterate of the 21st Century will not be those who cannot read and write. The illiterate of the 21st Century will be those who cannot learn, unlearn and relearn."

No matter who you are, what you do or how well you do it. You better be constantly looking for ways to get better, to change and to jettison old ways of doing business. Because as that business professor said so many years ago: "No business has a *right* to exist."

Simplicity: Not Oversimplifying

When I think about Simplicity, I'm afraid that many people immediately think we mean oversimplified. We're not talking about oversimplifying anything here. What we are saying is that everyone in your organization, and I mean every single person from the C-Suite to the frontline employees, must understand four things:

1. What is this goal we need everyone to maniacally focus on?
   a. What metric are we trying to improve?
   b. How much are we trying to improve it?
   c. By when are we trying to achieve it?
2. Why do we want to improve this goal?
3. What is the job to be done?
4. What is my part of this goal?

Think about this for a moment. Really think about it. Every goal of real consequence that you've ever achieved you had a really good idea about each of these aspects of the goal. No one just shows up at a major university and walks out with a degree a few weeks or months later. No one just shows up at Mount Everest and climbs it without any planning or preparation. No one just shows up on Broadway and stars in a musical without preparation. The list goes on and on. Les Brown puts it this way, "Not everything that's hard is worth doing, but everything worth doing is hard."

At Blaze, we know you can reduce the difficulty of the dive if you ensure that you and everyone in your organization truly understands and internalizes all four steps above. This is another reason we believe you can only have one overarching goal that any group or team is maniacally focused on.

Sometimes people tell us something like: "Our industry and business are very complex, and it is impossible to break it down to simple steps or requirements." If you don't break it down so simply that everyone can understand; what's the probability that they will consistently perform the ABCs required to achieve the goal?

Perhaps Albert Einstein said it best when he said: "The definition of genius is taking the complex and making it simple." Or, if you prefer a more recent perspective, consider Steve Jobs' statement: "Deciding what not to do is as important as deciding what to do."

We're not trying to say your business or your job to be done is simple, but we are saying that what you're trying to achieve must be outlined in such a way that there is no way anyone can misunderstand what they must focus on every single day. We are also saying that while your business is "different" (we hear that all the time) if you continue to do things the way you always have, then you can only expect the same results.

Dr. Robert Jarvik is the inventor of the first successful artificial heart. One day, an author interviewed him about his thoughts on leadership. During the interview, Dr. Jarvik was called out for an emergency while the author waited in his office. After a few moments, another man entered Dr. Jarvik's office and began cleaning the room and emptying the trash. When the author asked about his role within the organization, the gentleman described his job and contribution in this way: "Me and Dr. Jarvik, we save lives."

This story is a wonderful example of an employee knowing they were making an impact and a leader who created collaboration and empowerment! This man knew his job was essential to saving the lives of their patients. His work did not require an MD to perform, but it did require his best efforts every day. This is the epitome of Simplicity.

The Necessity of Visibility

One of the common mistakes is making what should be visible, hard to see. There are lots of reasons for this, but the fact is, unless your entire team works in the same room, it is hard to keep up with what everyone is doing. It's even harder keeping up with those powerful few ABCs that really move the needle. This is exactly why we created our Execution platform, EIYP **(Execution in Your Pocket®),** so you can see every day, all day, in real-time how every person is doing with those high leverage ABCs. No one in your organization should ever say again "I'm not making an impact" or "I'm not making a difference."

As a leader, I don't need to know everything that my team members are doing all day long, that's micromanaging. What we are talking about is tapping into the power of making the completion of the ABCs by every team member a formulaic, gamified system. It is a fact that we all play differently when we start keeping score. In this case, we're keeping score on the ABCs. If you've identified the right ABCs and you can see how consistently everyone is doing them, there is little doubt that your results are going to improve.

I say little doubt because the world could change on you and the things which used to get results don't work anymore. That is why it is even MORE important to ensure clear visibility of what everyone is doing. You don't want to keep doing the wrong things, hoping to get the right results. If the actions are wrong, you want to be able to course-correct quickly and adjust your ABCs to ensure success. One of the many advantages of utilizing EIYP ® is that you will know exactly how consistently everyone is doing the ABCs. You will know exactly how frequently people are doing the highest leverage activities to be successful in achieving the goals.

For most organizations, they have no idea how consistently people are doing these things.

EIYP® creates tremendous real-time visibility and metrics to lead your people and manage your business more effectively. Some time ago I was showing the CEO of a rapidly growing company some of this data and he was blown away. He said, "I knew there was a problem, but now I have data to back that up." In this day and age, we all need data to help us lead ourselves and others more effectively.

The ABCs are different for every job and every organization. When identifying the ABCs, it is essential to remember Edward Deming's Axiom, "If you want to understand cause and effect in any job you must talk to the person standing within 12 feet of the job." Specifically, this means that you cannot identify, with certainty, the ABCs for a group of people 3 or 4 levels below you in your organization. Just as you would not want the front-line employee telling the COO what to do, you need to be as close to the work as possible to decide the ABCs. At the moment, some of you are agreeing wholeheartedly and some of you are thinking "I've been here for 25 years and I used to have that job. I know exactly what their ABCs should be!"

I can understand this perspective but let's consider two questions:

1. Is it possible the job could have changed any since you had it?
2. Is it possible the people currently doing the job might have some valuable insights or ideas?

In your experience, which scenario creates more buy-in and engagement: Telling people what to do or getting their ideas and buy-in as you request their input? Let me give a personal example. A year ago, my adult daughter decided she wanted to start looking for a new car and asked for my help. I love cars and have owned more than fifty of them, so I was more than happy to help. In very short order I selected exactly the car (actually, an SUV) even down to the color to meet her requirements, needs and wants. She then admitted that she really appreciated my help but wanted to drive some different cars on her own.

Of course, I thought it was a great idea! After looking at several cars and driving a few of them she ultimately decided to get the car I recommended (she even loved the color I recommended). I then said something like, "I knew you would like it, and that's why I originally selected it as the best choice for you." She immediately replied, "I'm sorry I should have taken your word for it." I instantly regretted saying anything. She should not have felt sorry at all! This was 100% her choice and I was supposed to be helping her, not doing it for her. She paid for the car; she is the person who needs to love it and live with it. This was about her deciding what was right for her because she is the one that has to drive it every day.

When it comes to the ABCs, of course you should have some ideas, insights and maybe even input, but after decades of doing this, let me tell you in no uncertain terms, if you mandate without input it will fail. Your teams will not own the ABCs. They will be working on your orders, and if it doesn't work, it will be your fault.

What if the ABCs are Not Working

This leads to an important question we hear all the time: What if everyone is doing their ABCs but the results are not improving as expected? This is a rare but can be quite concerning. In most organizations we've worked with, there is no breakout of execution. The number of organizations that have everyone aligned and pulling in the same direction on the same goals is frightfully low. Having said that, what if your organization is the anomaly? What if you have everyone consistently recording in EIYP and reporting in your meetings that they're doing their ABCs and it's not moving the needle? What's going on? Well, in every case there are four possible reasons:

1. They're pencil whipping the ABCs

The first reason is self-explanatory, basically people are being dishonest and saying they're doing the work but they're not. If they're not doing the work of course you're not going to get the results. If you have people not being truthful in EIYP ® as well as in their team meetings you have a far bigger issue. If you have this problem, no amount of planning and Execution will get you the results you want. If you have this problem, you need your leaders to start leading and take responsibility for what their people are doing or not doing.

2. The ABCs need more time to work

Here's an easy way to describe the second issue. If I plant some apple seeds, I'm not going to get apples in a couple of months, it takes longer. No one wants to wait years for a tree to grow, but you do have to be realistic about whether you have a situation where it will take more than a few weeks or months to achieve. This is both art and science, you must give enough time to see real results and if you aren't, then it's time to reevaluate them.

It could also be that you need to do more of the ABCs. For example, let's say I want to lose ten pounds within two months. It will not happen if I only reduce my food intake by 100 calories per day with no increase in exercise. I might lose two pounds in two months, but not 10. In this case I need to increase how many ABCs I'm doing (how many calories I'm cutting out) and increase my exercise to burn off more calories. It's important to have a realistic view of what results will come from the actions, behaviors and commitments your team is doing.

3. Quality vs. Quantity

Some of our clients are professional services firms (in this case, Law Firms and Accounting Firms). In every case, they would like to get their lawyers and accountants to schedule more face to face meetings with their clients and prospective clients. Why? Because they want them to keep the clients they currently have, identify more business opportunities with them, and find new clients as well. If their people are not consistently having these kinds of meetings, the first step is to get them in the habit of scheduling and holding these face-to-face meetings. As they more consistently hold these meetings, you can also focus on the quality of the meetings. Are they asking the right questions? Are they focusing on identifying the needs of the client and so forth, rather than just getting together to shoot the breeze? In every organization you need people to do the right ABCs and do them well. You need both the right quantity and good quality.

4. The Wrong ABCs

Quite frankly, we have not seen #4 very often with our clients. In some cases, the world has dramatically changed, and the organization and people are stuck in the past, working on the wrong ABCs. But we see this less than any of the other issues. If this is the case it quickly becomes apparent. Because if everyone is completing their ABCs consistently over time and nothing is happening, you know there is another problem. The issue is that most organizations cannot measure how consistently their people are doing the ABCs. They can identify how the results or outcomes are going but they don't have a way to see the ABCs in real-time. That's just one of the reasons EIYP ® is such an essential tool for any organization that is trying to get their people aligned and pulling together on their goals.

Visibility – The ABCs – Making the Vital Visible

There are as many different goals as there are organizations. Many years ago, when we were still pretty new at helping organizations execute strategies to achieve their goals, I had the VP of Operations for an electrical equipment company tell me something I will never forget. He said he didn't think we could help him because we had not done any work with an electrical equipment manufacturer. I had to laugh because one of my partners and I both spent several years in manufacturing. I immediately replied that he was correct, we had not worked in his industry. This did not change the fact that just like every other business I've seen before or since, he had the same issues. He needed his people to consistently complete a series of ABCs to create a product, deliver a service or product or any number of other things.

It's interesting to note that in the fifteen years since that conversation, we have worked in healthcare, retail, trucking, hospitality, heavy manufacturing, light manufacturing, finance, insurance, state and federal government, and too many others to mention. We've found that no matter the industry, success still boils down to getting employees to consistently do the right things, ideally without you having to hover over them. While there are definitely various nuances and cultures to navigate, the issue and its resolution are typically similar.

In every industry, I can imagine the way they do business has changed dramatically over the last five to ten years. In many industries there has been huge upheaval in just the last five to ten months. Now more than ever you need to ensure every employee truly understands which goal they must focus on.

In hospitals, there is a huge push for decreasing the number of patients who return to the hospital for the same health issues. These are called "re-admits." It is a metric they are measured on and insurers reimburse more or less money based on how well the hospital is doing. The problem is there are hundreds of things healthcare workers are responsible for every day. If they are not crystal clear on the ABCs (Activities, Behaviors and Commitments) necessary for every patient interaction there are going to be re-admits.

A large landscape chemical company we worked with wanted to obtain and retain more customers. They realized that the technicians who sprayed the chemicals on their customers' property were the literal face of the company. Quite frankly, these techs were so busy they thought their only job was to spray the chemicals on the yard and move on to the next job. But what if they could get the techs to start thinking of themselves as customer service reps who called the customers by name, verified the work to be done and verified the company had their credit card on file so they would not have to worry about billing. As the techs began to think this way, they got excited about the new recognition of their importance to the success of the company. Many even started hanging company flyers on a few houses and businesses they were spraying to drum up more business. That kind of engagement goes straight to the bottom line.

It was these kinds of activities and excitement that helped the business grow by nearly 25% within a couple of months. Far more importantly, they had empowered and excited their lawn techs, who started to understand, in a whole new way, how important their work was to the company's growth and success. They understood they were more than just a warm body spraying chemicals: they were customer service and sales reps who were really making a difference.

So often people don't perform the way we hope because they're not sure what to do or how to do it. Or even worse what they've been doing is not working or getting the results you or they want, and they're stuck with no way to get out.

At the Lawn Chemical Company, they were smart enough to ask several of the most successful lawn techs what they were doing to be successful. They came up with some really great ideas (like hanging the flyers on the doors of the nearby homes and businesses). When you're trying to identify the best ABCs for any group of people you want to get some ideas and input from the people currently doing the job. Even if you already know exactly what to do, we know your people and teams will benefit from being part of the process of identifying the ABCs for success.

Here's another example of this in action. When I was a kid, there was this great department store which had great products. A friend of mine worked with their women's shoe departments to help them grow sales, specifically by increasing sales per transaction. In other words, they wanted each salesperson to sell more shoes to each customer. As he talked to their best salespeople, he found they consistently did 3 things:

1. When a customer asked to try on a pair of shoes, they would ask them a little about what work they did and how they would use the shoes.

2. They would always bring out one or two additional pairs of shoes which the woman might find interesting and relevant for their needs (the needs they had just asked about).

3. They would ask the customer if they would like to charge the shoes on their store branded department store charge card? If they didn't have charge card, they would offer to open one for them instantly.

I bet you can see where this is going and have probably seen it in the retail world today. Very few department stores were using this approach at the time, and when those professional shoe salespeople began consistently applying these ideas, it was truly revolutionary. Rarely were salespeople consistently doing these 3 things.

Now think about it, if the salesperson brings out extra shoes, which fit the needs of the customer, they are a lot more likely to sell more than just the original pair the customer asked for. Here's another interesting fact: The employees of the store knew that if customers charged on their credit card, they would likely spend more than twice as much as they would with cash or their own credit card (Zero interest strikes again).

By the way, as they implemented these ABCs with the salespeople in multiple shoe departments, they saw dramatic increases in sales in every store. The consistent application of these practices (ABCs) helped them become so successful they were eventually purchased by a competitor. In the meantime, everyone made more money.

David, who is a co – author of this book, understands the ABCs mindset in a most incredible way. Over his career, by partnering with his teams, he has implemented ABCs which fundamentally changed the way those organizations where he worked did business.

The first example is when he was COO for a large concrete block manufacturer. The company had a multi-million dollar piece of equipment. This piece of equipment was not working. Every single day there was unplanned downtime and they were missing customer shipments. The sales team was getting frustrated. So upset, they were openly blaming the production team for all the company's issues.

David met with the production team and just asked the simple question, 'How is the preventative maintenance going on our production equipment?' Stunned, the plant manager, said, 'We don't have time for preventative maintenance – we have to keep the machine running so we can meet the production schedule!' David in his straightforward approach said, 'Really? We don't have time to take care of the equipment which is making money for us? But, we have time to scrap bad product, because we didn't take time to do it right the first time. Nice.'

After, a couple more meetings, the team decided to create the goal, which was, *reduce unplanned downtime to less than 1 hour a week so we can make the sales team and our customers happy.* Notice the why, and the production team was very serious about making internal and external customers happy.

One of the ABCs, was radical in its approach. David led the charge on this because he knew there would be a huge gasp of air when it would be revealed. The radical ABC was, every Monday, the entire plant would shut down and every piece of equipment would have preventative maintenance performed on it.   Can you see the mind blowing emoji taking place when David revealed the ABC to the entire organization?   He was making the call to reduce production time by 20% so as to meet shipments to customers! Mind-blowing!

IT WORKED! By taking the time to take care of the equipment they were able to increase production output. Because they were able to increase production, they were able to ship on time.

The ABC of performing preventative maintenance every Monday, was the most critical driver of David's team achieving the goal.

Every Monday, people knew, machines would be down, being thoroughly overhauled, to make sure customer shipments would be made on time.   Eventually, the production team was able to reduce the hours of preventative maintenance work from 8 hours to 4 hours and they were able to start producing product on Monday afternoons.

The ABCs was one of the Keys which helped unlock Execution and propelled David's team to success. It was that simple.

The second example where the ABCs played a critical role in helping David and his team achieve their goal was when he accepted the leadership role for manufacturing operations of a large electronic contract manufacturer in the Carolinas.

David met with leadership and they came up with a goal to be the cleanest (based on the company's audit system and what the team called NASCAR shop clean) manufacturing facility in this 200,000 plus employee organization so they could reduce employee turnover and increase on time delivery. You are thinking, 'What!? How can a clean plant reduce employee turnover AND increase on time delivery to clients?'

We asked the same question at Blaze because we could not connect the dots. David explained it to us by saying, 'A clean plant brings pride to the people who are working there – they take pride in how clean things are. They enjoy working in a clean environment. The better organized the plant the easier it is to see the flow of product in the plant and the less likelihood, parts will get lost in the manufacturing process and the less likelihood someone would get hurt.'

It worked!

Every ABC was created to ensure the plant was clean. David did not create the ABCs for the team. The team created them and then the team held each other accountable to make sure the ABCs were acted on **daily.**

One of the ABCs was as simple as, if something is sitting on the floor, it needs to be in a painted square. Every tool has its place every tool has its space.

David told us he knew the team had achieved success not when just the goals were met, but when an employee brought his family to the plant to show it off because she was so proud of it. David walked with the family and the children just kept saying, this place is so clean!

By the way, the place was a sheet metal fabrication and integration facility. Not exactly an easy place to keep clean with all the sheet metal grinding, sanding and painting, but the team did it. Why? Because they knew their ABCs.

The last story we will tell about David, when it comes to running the *3 Keys of Execution*, was when he was part owner of a large hospitality staffing company. David took on the responsibility to opening up a new market for his company. The market was Orlando, Florida.

Here is the irony, of this story. One of his customers was a 3000 plus room property, can you say, 'Bon Voyage?' If you can read in between the lines, you know the hotel brand. Anyway, this staffing customer used to be a client of his when he was doing consulting work for another company. So here we have, the teacher with the student?

Kung Fu if you will – Grasshopper with the teacher. What would happen?

This hotel property loved David when he did consulting work with them, but what did David know about housekeeping staffing? Nothing. Because of them 'liking' David in a past role, they thought they would give him a chance. The chance began with providing 10 housekeepers for their hotel.

David ran a simpler version of Execution in his head (one of the many thoughts we used at Blaze to develop the *3 Keys* over the last 3 years) and he broke the challenges of the job down by taking the time to understand from the housekeepers **THEIR ABCs**! By listening to them on what they needed to do, to get the job done and what he needed to do to have them promote the company to friends and family, they came up with goal and their ABCs. The goal was to reduce turnover so as to increase sales and provide jobs for family and friends (this is groundbreaking just this goal alone.) Their ABCs were simple:

1. Correct all payroll issues within 24 hours (yes, they would overnight a check for just a $1.00 to make sure the housekeeper knew they were serious about their pay)

2. Make sure all cleaning carts were properly staged and supplied one hour before shift

started (housekeepers don't like unexpected OT)

3. Engage each new employee for the first 90 days daily with a quick check in and then have a scheduled weekly meeting for 10 minutes (or more if needed) just to make sure they were feeling supported and cared for by the team

Pretty simple and straightforward.

By following this process, David's Team grew the market from 0 to over 200 housekeepers in less than a year or close to $8 million in revenue. A true testament to the work this team in Orlando was verbalized when another client of David's from his previous consulting days was engaged in the following conversation.

The client was and is the USA's largest valet parking service. The Senior Executive asked this hotel, where David's Team was providing housekeeping services, what did the valet parking company need to do to provide the best service this hotel has or could ever get. The valet executive asked this question expecting to hear the answer, 'Well, there is nothing your company can do, because you are providing the best service.' Guess what? He did not hear the answer he was expecting to get. What he heard was, 'Matt, if you could provide service like David

Williams' team, then you would be providing the best service anyone could provide.' His mouth dropped.

We share these stories to not point out our team members' success, we share these stories to point out two critical points:

1. Execution is a straightforward process

2. If you make things complicated, you will not be successful

Because of David's mastery of *The 3 Keys*, he was able to effectively lead organizations which made concrete block, high end electronics and led an organization which provided housekeeping services. David went to the people who could answer the questions! Who were those people? The ones closest to the problem. The ones who would ultimately be tasked with executing on the ABCs.

Visibility – The Offense can see what the Defense is doing

If you think about great teams and great organizations, they know they can count on each other. If you play any sport, you can see what everyone else on the field or floor is doing. If you play in a band, you know what the other musicians are doing. If you're in a play or musical there is no hiding your performance on stage. If you are on a

NASCAR racing team you can certainly see what the driver and the entire crew is doing during the race.

On the best teams everyone is watching and knows what is going well and what is not.

Why don't we do this in business and other organizations? Most of the time it's because unless you work in close proximity to each other, you have no way of seeing or knowing what's going on with the other team members. This is why our dynamic, gamified platform, Execution in Your Pocket® (EIYP), is so essential to your success. It allows you and everyone (from the C-Suite to the Front Line) to see real time the ABCs of every person. There is no hiding and there is a lot of celebrating (just like in a successful game, performance or race).

Just a few minutes ago, when I was making my 5-minute daily update in EIYP ® for my ABCs on our team I saw two high-fives from one of my team members who lives in another state. No matter who you are its kind of cool to get a high-five for doing something well. I don't think you ever outgrow that kind of recognition.

The 3 Keys of Execution and the ABCs

Another relevant consideration when creating a culture of execution is the fire that is most often buried deep inside. James Morrison, a good friend of mine once told me, "This exceptional trait is best illustrated in inspired hope and a desire to live life beyond the mundane and natural flow of life. Those who capture the sheer essence of this intangible quality discover the ability to make everything POSSIBLE! The differentiation between mediocre and excellent is none other than GRIT."

Grit is determination, perseverance, tenacity and courage. It is the resistance to never give up. Successful organizations are ultimately successful because of the GRIT of their people! GRIT at Blaze is epitomized with the ABCs!

Unfortunately, the importance of really understanding the ABCs needed to win the game is often lost due to the agonizing attempt to understand the job to be done! Employees need to understand the strategic direction and the purpose of their contribution. A meaningful connection is useful to help persuade others to give when everything is exhausted. The *3 Keys of Execution* is the connector between an individual's desire to win and the job to be done! The ABCs—the GRIT, if you will—is how the goal is achieved!

How the ABCs help your organization when set free by the 3 Keys of Execution

Execution is the difference between failure and success. The ABCs are the difference of 1 degree, between 211 and 212 degrees—that extra one degree turns hot water into boiling water, which generates steam, which as we know powers so much in our world. A little improvement of one degree of activity and measurement can provide exponential results. The ABCs dramatically increase the possibility of achieving that one extra degree. One inch will score the winning touchdown or conversely, one inch could lose the game. The ABCs are the mental and physical determination to do something which produces extraordinary benefit.

The challenge becomes the motivation to keep going when everything has been exhausted. When everything seems vulnerable and ominous, even at the hands of the most extenuating circumstances and challenges, it's the ABCs that keep the human and organizational spirit alive to bear the adversity. Why? Because the ABCs are those things which will lead us to victory!

There are some things that need to be stripped away for the human spirit to be nurtured and to have momentum. For example, the common conditions of a poor culture suppress the will to give more, to give beyond what is required. To do this, it's necessary to understand all the organizational relationships of reward systems, leadership styles, business goals, rapid access to information, examining the conscious and unconscious value system and much more. People behave in perfect alignment to the system they are required to work in. The best environments are those where there is mutual benefit for the INDIVIDUAL, TEAM and ORGANIZATION. It must be noted that individual motivation or reward is not just monetary, but rather seeing and comprehending how their contribution adds value.

A poor execution culture suppresses the one point of measurement, it prevents the one-degree increase in temperature; it stops the players one inch short. Similarly, it turns this valuable opportunity from a success to an "Almost Did It" speech. How many of us want to reduce the number of organizational hurdles employees must work through to get the job done? We all do! Enhancing the ability of an organization to become an execution culture is not an easy task.

As the power of execution grows, it produces greater excitement to not only to do what is expected but also to reach the seemingly unachievable. Hope is one of the intangibles impacting performance. Hope powers execution to place blind men on Mount Everest, paraplegics across the marathon finish line and all sorts of other heroic and inspirational stories. The conditions to give up, throw in the towel, to say "I can't do it," can be stopped when exposed to INDIVIDUALS, TEAMS and ORGANIZATIONS who understand their purpose.

Participants often play the game by offering their talents, skill, knowledge and attributes; they play the game because of the competitive nature to win. Nobody likes sitting on the bench, they want to be in the game giving it their best! Make the move to tap into purpose and meaning by opening immense opportunities by creating an execution culture.

The Curse of Mediocrity

Think about how the times you have received mediocre service. Sometimes we get so accustomed to mediocrity that we begin to make it acceptable. When you think about execution as a system of *3 Keys*, simplicity, visibility and accountability, there is no hiding. There is no room for mediocrity. When you have an execution culture you have to perform.

Let's do a quick review of the *3 Keys*. The first key is **simplicity**. Everyone understands (in clear and simple terms): What the goal is, why it's important, the job to be done and the ABCs they need to be accomplishing.

Because you have Simplicity you can now have **visibility,** because we know the goals and the ABCs for achieving the goal. We can now have 100% transparency. Everybody in the organization has committed to helping us achieve the goal and we are putting that information into Execution In Your Pocket® which everyone can see.

Now that you have visibility, you can now have **accountability**. Why?

Because everybody knows what everybody is doing from the CEO to the front line. Because you have this execution system in place, there is no longer any room for mediocrity. People can no longer hide because the data will indicate who is performing and who is not.

Several years ago, in a manufacturing facility in North Carolina, I was giving an annual performance review to a member of my team. Let's call her Julie. I asked the question, "What is the one thing that you are most proud of over this last year that you have done to really make a difference in this organization?"

Julie looked me right in the eye and she said, "The thing that I am most proud of is that I have perfected the art of mediocrity, and people have mistaken it for excellence." My jaw dropped. I was her boss. I was giving her a performance review, and she sat there and basically indicated she had pulled the wool over everyone's eyes!

This is a person who had an undergraduate degree from the University of North Carolina Chapel Hill and a Master's from Clemson University. I was astounded. As you can imagine, within 6 months she was no longer working for our organization.

Do you have team members who have grown so accustom to mediocrity that they mistake it for excellence? If this is the case you don't have Simplicity, Visibility and Accountability in place.

The Art of Accountability

Many decades ago one popular management approach was called MBE or Management by Exception. The idea was simple, as a leader you constantly scanned your team or organization looking for any underperforming areas, teams or people (exceptions). The goal was to manage them back into acceptable performance. One of the problems with this approach was you missed a lot of other opportunities because the focus was on the exceptions rather than where you should be heading.

In the 1980s there was a big shift to MBO (Management by Objective). The idea with this approach was that you would identify the strategic goals and objectives and manage performance to achieving them. The hope was that as the exceptions or outliers saw everyone else moving forward, they would follow their lead. Sometimes they did and sometimes they gave up along the way. One of the problems with MBO is something called "Scope Creep" in project management jargon. That is, if 3 goals or objectives are good then maybe five or six would be better. If six are good, how much better could we be if we achieve twelve critical goals? Very quickly you have so many important goals that no one can keep up. There may be no faster way to becoming a Jack of All trades and Master of None than trying to do everything and assuming everything is equally important. If *everything* is important, then *nothing* is important.

What we're proposing here is that if you want this year to be fundamentally different than last year you have to do fundamentally different things. So far in this book we've asked you to simplify by selecting one goal you will maniacally focus on this year and make everyone's performance of the ABCs visible to everyone (C-Suite to the Front-Line). Now we want you to do the same thing with Accountability.

We're not talking about annual or quarterly performance reviews. Think for a moment about the coach of an athletic team or the director of a play or musical production. In either case, how soon after a game or a performance will that coach or director wait to talk with their people about their performances? In many cases it will be immediately afterwards or at a minimum the next day or two. Can you imagine any coach or director saying "Great job out there! I'll talk with you at the end of the year." Of course not, that sounds ludicrous. Any coach or director will talk to his people instantly. If he doesn't, how likely is his team to win? Or even get better? Not very!

When you think about helping yourself and your team get better, you can see why we make such a big deal about weekly and daily accountability on every team in your organization. If we wait for weeks or months to check back with people, there might be some improvement but who knows what you will see. We're also saying that every single person should be able to see that everyone else is doing the same thing day in and day out (accomplishing their ABCs that is).   Our Execution in Your Pocket (EIYP) ® gamified tool allows you to do exactly this. It allows everyone to see what everyone else is actually doing with their ABCs.

The fact is, that the only people who want to hide are those who are *not* performing.   Think about it. If you're doing your job you may not want your picture on the website, but you don't want to hide the fact that you're doing your job either.

Most people really do want to perform well! Many times, they don't because they don't know how to, or they're so busy doing "stuff" they never move to the next level. They need a great coach or director to help them.

I have seen it again and again, in organizations large and small. People tend to rise to the level of expectation.   I know of a business leader who complains that he has very high turnover and that his people are lazy and poor performers.   Unfortunately, he treats them like they are lazy and untrustworthy.   And, in true self-fulfilling prophecy fashion, people don't stay. As you would expect, the best employees leave first. Who wants to stick around and put up with that sort of abuse?

This is the opposite of what we recommend when it comes to Accountability, but it does take some work, commitment and absolute consistency. Consistency of what? Consistency of following the *3 Keys of Execution*:

1. **Ensure that every person knows exactly what the goal is and their piece of it – Simplicity.**
2. **Ensure that every person can see that everyone is doing their part – Visibility.**
3. **Have every person account to their team (daily and weekly) their completion of their ABCs. – Accountability.**

Accountability Killer - Diffusion of Responsibility

In the world of professional Psychology, "Diffusion of Responsibility" is the phenomenon of a person being less likely to take responsibility for action when others are present. My grandfather used to say, "The fastest way to starve a horse is to give it two masters." Basically, he meant that if you assign (diffuse) responsibility to more than one person, it is more likely that neither will do the task. Each person will instead tell himself that the other person will take care of it. The problem here, of course, is that if both people believe that the other will take care of the task and neither completes it, then the task will never be executed.

Another example of this would be the field goal kicker missing the extra points and blaming the other team's fans for being too loud. Or the actor on the stage forgetting lines and blaming it on a crying child in the audience. No one is perfect, but if we allow the poor performance of others to relinquish our responsibility for our performance, we have a problem.

In the business world we see this all the time. We create great goals and beautiful strategies and prepare to hit it out of the park, yet at the end of the quarter or the year, we see that our goals were not met. Why does this happen? Too often, we see this happen because the formula of execution was not followed. The goal was not simple, actions were not visible and there was no accountability in place to ensure it was followed. Every missed step in this formula will lead to reduced success or even failure. One of the key elements of creating a culture of Accountability is to ensure there is no Diffusion of Responsibility.

While the concept of Diffusion of Responsibility is simple to understand and see in real life, it can be difficult to negate in organizational environments. In order to do this, you must not only effectively clarify the goals, but also the roles that are associated with the execution and completion of each goal. Most organizational goals are not single-person efforts, they are group, and in most cases multi-group, efforts. This requires effective communication among disparate organizational groups.

An example would be the implementation of a new CRM tool. It takes the collaboration of several groups, like IT, Sales, perhaps Analytics and Customer Service. Getting the system up is not really the goal here, it is to have team members using the system effectively and harnessing the power of the CRM. While all these teams are involved, they are not all responsible for every facet of the implementation and execution. Therefore, it is key for the teams to understand, with the utmost clarity, how their roles in the process are integral to the success of the project.

I would recommend leaders be leery of assigning project tasks to whole teams, such as "Sales is responsible for developing the training of the tool". This is where we see "Diffusion of Responsibility" come into play the most. Each member on the Sales team then thinks that someone else will handle the development of the training, but it doesn't take place. An effective way to negate this effect is to ensure that each assignment is given a single name, a single point of responsibility that will have their name and reputation attached to its completion. This increased visibility and accountability will lend itself to ensuring that no task goes unnoticed, each task and its importance is highlighted to the entire team.

If we expand our view from the project realm into the organizational goal realm it is imperative that you do not lose the concept of single points of responsibility. Increasing revenue by 15% is a great goal and, for many companies, would be a stretch goal for a year; however, trying to meet this goal by simply saying "sales team, go sell more" will not lead to the result you are looking for. It is important to effectively cascade the goal so that each member of the Sales team understands exactly what their role in the greater goal is and how their individual actions will positively impact the goal. This means that each sales representative will be able to precisely identify how many calls/sales/meetings/new clients/etc. They MUST achieve to hit the target. As you cascade the *3 Keys of Execution* with *Execution In Your Pocket*® you will also see that the Visibility they create will be critically important to the success of hitting the goal. One thing is certain, we say it multiple times in this book—people play differently when you keep score.

Accountability – Communication

A huge part of accountability begins with effective communication. Have you ever practically killed yourself to get something done for someone only to have them tell you that was not what they wanted? Or maybe you've made an assignment and received something very different than what you expected.

This reminds me of the story about the second grader who came home from school and asked his mom where he came from. She thought to herself *"I never thought I would have to discuss the birds and the bees with my seven-year-old son!"* But he asked, so she began by telling him that it all started when she met his dad and fell in love. They decided to get married and have children. She then went into some detail about how she got pregnant and carried him in her stomach for nine months and that, when he was born, it was one of the happiest days of their lives.

After her careful explanation the little boy looked a little bewildered and responded, "Well, Sarah told me she came from Nebraska, and I was wondering where I came from."

> **It has been said that the biggest problem with communication is the assumption that it occurred.**

How often has someone told you something, and after you asked a few questions, you found out that what you thought you understood was not at all what they meant?

Part of the problem here is that the same words mean different things to different people. For example, what do you think of when I say, "I just bought a boat?" Some of you immediately think of a fishing boat to take out early

Saturday morning. Some of you imagine a ski boat, others a canoe, and still others a big cabin cruiser to take on the ocean. Isn't it funny how one four letter word can mean so many different things to different people?

What if I say, "My son wants us to get a dog"? Some of you will remember happy days with your dog growing up. That dog could have been a Collie, a Poodle, a German Shephard, or my neighbor's Great Dane (which is more like a small horse). Even the 3-letter word *dog* evokes very different images in people's minds.

Is it any wonder that communication can be so difficult? We cannot assume people understand what we mean just because we tell them.

It's even more difficult when you add in the complexity of different languages, or even different ages, genders and ethnicities. None of which are bad but do add some interesting dynamics to effective communication.

When it comes to accountability and achieving your goals, you must be sure everyone knows what you really mean and want. They have to understand not only the *what, when* and *where*, but also the *why*.

Take a moment and think of someone you know or have read about who is (or was) a very effective communicator. What made them so effective? Are you doing the things they did to be effective? If not, why? It's hard and it takes time, but the fact is, if you don't have time to communicate well the first time, when will you have time to do it better later?

The next time you need to communicate to your teammates, kids, friends (or anyone else for that matter) take a moment to consider 3 questions you want answered when you're done talking:

1. What do you want them to know?
2. What do you want them to do?
3. What do you want them to feel?

If you will slow down just a bit and think through these 3 questions, you will be able to crystalize your message and dramatically increase the probability of them understanding the message. In other words, you've effectively communicated. Of course, a huge part of this is also taking some time to let them ask questions and ensure they really understand what you want them to know, do and feel. Yes, this takes a little time, but is it better to skip these essential steps and leave them thinking you're talking about a fishing boat when you really need a cruise ship?

Accountability and Integrity

This is how you make this year the best one ever. This is the secret sauce. As well as you might do with the first two Keys, if you don't consistently hold everyone, and we mean *everyone*, accountable, you will not achieve nearly the amount of success as you might otherwise. On every successful athletic team, they not only have first string players but second, third, and fourth string players who are expected to know the plays and excel at them. In every play or musical, there are understudies who can take over if the lead actors cannot perform. This is why you must have everyone participating.

You never know when someone will step up and become your next Leader.

As you already know, for Accountability to work, you need to meet with your team. For those who work in the same location, this can be easier. Many of the teams I've led over the last 15 years have been spread out over multiple locations; this makes accountability a challenge, but it is still possible. Here are a few things we know work.

Everyone on the team must explain in 60 – 90 seconds their answers to these questions:

1. What ABCs did I accomplish vs what I said I would do?
2. Do I need help?
3. What's next?

In my experience, the more they say, the less they did. That's right, you don't want people to drone on giving lots of explanations or excuses. You want them to quickly and concisely tell what they did or did not do. This is why the 60 – 90 second time limit is so important. This is also not the place for the leader to give lots of feedback (especially if tough feedback is required). Remember the old axiom: "Praise in public; correct in private."

Another recommendation is to rotate who leads the meeting every time you meet. Whomever leads the meeting also reports first on how they did with their ABCs, whether they need help and what's next? By rotating the leadership of the meeting everyone on the team begins to understand what it means to try and get the entire team moving.

My friend tells the story of working with the president of a company who was holding his first weekly meeting with his direct reports. Each of them was an executive who was responsible for their own locations with 100s of employees and millions of dollars in monthly revenue. In the first meeting, the president reported his progress and asked the other executives to report on their ABCs. The next executive to report, admitted that it had been a very busy week and he had not accomplished his ABCs. Every leader after him gave essentially the same report. At the end of this very public lack of performance the president asked everyone if they understood how important this was? Not only had they not kept their word to him and each other, they had set a very poor example for all their employees. He went on to say, if we cannot do what we say we'll do, how can we possibly expect everyone else to do what they say they'll do? Everyone apologized and committed that they would complete their ABCs that week.

Seven days later, in their next meeting. The president began the meeting again by sharing his accomplishment of his ABCs and proceeded to ask the next leader about his performance. After a nervous laugh this leader gave the excuse that he had been incredibly busy and had not completed his ABCs. The President chose to hold his tongue (planning on correcting in private) and went on to the next leader. This leader spoke about traveling on business and not completing the ABCs. The President then asked the leader if they had known they would be traveling when they committed to the ABCs the previous week. They had to admit that they did know about the travel and should have planned better. Unfortunately for this president, the entire team had much the same excuses as to why they had not completed their ABCs.

As you can imagine, this president was not pleased with the performance of his team. Perhaps they didn't think the goal they were working on was important? Perhaps they thought the things they were doing were more important than their ABCs? Who knows?

At the end of this very visible lack of accomplishment, by every single leader, the president stopped, removed his glasses and said very calmly:

> I hope you all know that I love you and that I'm going to miss each one of you. A few weeks ago, we identified one goal that we all agreed we would maniacally focus on each week. We have all made commitments to our own ABCs to accomplish that goal. I have not told you what to select; you have chosen them. For the 2nd week in a row each of you shared how you let other things keep you from doing the things you said you would do, on the one goal we agreed required our maniacal focus. You are the senior executives of our firm, and *if* I cannot rely on you to do your part, how can I, in good conscience, expect anyone else to do better? To me this is a clear lack of integrity, and I cannot work with people who do not have integrity.

As you can imagine his entire team was stunned and immediately begged for mercy or forgiveness or whatever you want to call it and promised to do better.

We're certainly not recommending this over the top approach to accountability. But we are saying that if everyone does understand the importance of the goal and their essential part of it, then we should also be able to expect each other to complete our own ABCs on a daily or weekly basis.

Fortunately, the executive team in our story did go on to improve dramatically and create commitment and excitement throughout their organization which helped them achieve their goal like never before.

I do want to reinforce that we're not trying to intimidate anyone. We are trying to get you to be an effective coach or director to help your team or cast accomplish the goals you've agreed are most important to you.

My business partner, David is maniacal about this aspect of Accountability. He will tell leaders, you can have the worst ABCs known to mankind, but if you have your daily reviews and weekly accountability meetings, you will quickly figure out the ABCs are not quite good enough and then what happens next is true effectiveness.

The team begins to ask the question, 'What can I do better or different today, which will yield better results than what I had yesterday?' By having these consistent daily engagements, course correction will take place. People do not wake up in the morning, look themselves in the mirror and say, 'I want to be a loser!' People want to contribute and they want to contribute to a winning team! They want to belong!

Too many times leaders, put more emphasis on the ABCs rather than the purpose of *The 3 Keys of Execution*. The engagement piece of *The 3 Keys* is the purpose piece. It is where the belonging piece comes to life - if, and only if during the **engagement piece, the accountability piece is done correctly.** People need to understand how they fit into the whole scheme of things. People need to be able to choose their ABCs on what they are going to do to improve performance.

We, as human beings, have an insatiable need to understand and KNOW we belong to something. When you as a leader dictate the methods on how to achieve the goal, or only focus on the verbiage of the ABCs, you are taking away the individual's only opportunity (yes ONLY opportunity) to feel like they are part of something bigger than them AND when you dictate the methods, understand you have sucked the life out of the engagement piece.

When the team gets together to discuss how they are doing and what they are doing to move the needle on the organization's goals, this is their time to shine, contribute and understand how they are making a difference. This is the team's time to determine IF they are doing the right things. If they are your things, all they will say is, 'This is what I was told to do' AND they will keep doing it EVEN when it doesn't get the results. Why? Because the boss told me to!

Accountability: It's my Pleasure

When it comes to accountability, we often think it's something you do *to* people. We have found that the most powerful and consistent accountability, is when people are truly committed to the goal—when they believe in what they're doing. Did Mother Theresa need the Cardinal to hold her accountable? Did Michael Jordan need his coach Phil Jackson to push him in practice or in a game?

We believe, at our very core, that real accountability occurs when you first have simplicity and visibility. Meaning when people really understand the goal, why the goal is important and their part of the goal; and when everyone in the organization (from the C-Suite to the Frontline) can see that everyone is completing their ABCs daily and weekly. When they know that everyone else is on the hook too, accountability becomes something people start to own on a very personal level. This creates that Chick-fil-A and Ritz Carlton kinds of accountability. When every employee says, "It's my Pleasure" (Chick-fil-A) or acts like "Ladies and Gentlemen, serving Ladies and Gentlemen" (Ritz Carlton), you're creating a *real* culture of execution.

It has often been said that you can buy people's hands and backs, but you cannot buy their hearts and minds. This is what we're talking about. When everyone knows the team is counting on them and that no one else can or will do their important work for them; this is when you have people and teams who will run through brick walls to achieve your goals.

Accountability-An Equal Opportunity Employer

Several years ago, I was watching the College Football National Championship game and heard the announcer tell an interesting story. He said that earlier that day the two team captains met with the head coach to tell him they were sending two players home who had broken the rules. They would not be playing in the championship game. I don't know what that meeting was like, but this is truly amazing accountability. This was not the defensive coordinator telling two players to go home, nor was it another coach; it was the team captains, fellow players, who were enforcing the rules and monitoring the behaviors of their team members. As I recall, the two players sent home were excellent, and would have been a real asset to their team in the game. They would be watching the championship game from their parents' homes instead of the stadium. The team captains did the right thing and held their team members accountable for their ABCs (Actions, Behaviors and Commitments).

I am not saying we should send people home but think of the power it would create if every person in your organization, not only knows what they should be doing, but is holding themselves, and their team members, to this standard of personal accountability! You cannot help but see improved results!

By the way, this team became national champions that day because everyone else stepped up to fill the gap left by the two players who were sent home.

Conclusion

As we conclude this book, I am reminded of a quote by Mark Twain: "The secret to getting ahead is getting started."

You may not be able to implement 100% of what we've told you in this book by tomorrow. But pick one or two things you will start with and schedule those right now! Start with something. If I had to tell you to choose just one thing start at the beginning. Start with simplicity. Specifically, start with your goal and why it's important to you. Throughout human history people have overcome incredible odds because they understood *why* they were doing something! Ensuring that everyone understands that "why" is essential to your success.

You'll recall our discussion of Florence Chadwick, whose attempt to swim from Catalina Island to the California Coast ended just one mile short of triumph. "If I could have seen it, I could have made it." she said, after swimming for 15 hours and 55 minutes through the fog before ultimately quitting.

Two months later, Florence tried the swim again. The fog and weather were virtually the same as that first attempt on July 4th, but she kept swimming anyway. After 13 hours and 47 minutes she walked out of the water onto the California Coast, breaking a 27-year-old record by more than two hours, and becoming the first woman to ever complete the swim. This is such a great story about perseverance and keeping your eye on the goal.

This entire book has been focused on helping you, your team, and everyone you know continually see the goal and focus on their ABCs. All you need to be effective when it comes to Execution, are the *3 Keys*, Execution In Your Pocket®, and a servant leadership approach

Deeper Thinking: Creating a Culture of Execution

What does it take for an organization to create a culture of execution?

It's about **speed**—the ability to move fast to create and deliver goods and services to the general public.

If you are not competitive in purchasing, assembling, customer service, decision-making and efficiency, you WILL lose! You must always be thinking "highest quality at the lowest cost," which means manufacturing products and delivering services in the most efficient and effective way with the shortest lead-time.

Is your organization able to outperform your competition? A big part of this answer is how well you enable flexibility and versatility to meet the demands of the changing environment. If your organization isn't creating the marketing curve, then you are already going out of business. If you are not creating the marketing curve, it is probably because of a corporate structure that strangles innovation and execution!

Most organizations, regardless of size (headcount or revenue) are bloated with bureaucracy, forcing employees to jump through hoops to accomplish simple tasks. How many businesses are struggling because no one can make a move until the greatest authority gives their blessing? This type of hierarchy is no different for the CEO leading a multimillion-dollar organization or a proprietor managing a five and dime store. Thousands of organizations are slowly dying because of hierarchical constraints; meanwhile, the employees of the organization are left to their own devices.

The Sears Tower is a perfect case in point of the bureaucratic hierarchy of layered management, systems and processes. The hundred-story tower alongside Lake Michigan in Chicago, was once the ideal bureaucratic structure of corporate America. In contrast, the world headquarters for Wal-Mart in Benton, Arkansas is a flat building and, comparatively speaking, a rather flat organization. Bureaucratic organizations are sluggish, lethargic and exhausting; while non-tower organizations tend to be fast, agile and nimble.

Consider this example: A business has a problem with a customer order. Jane Doe, the customer service manager, is notified of a mix up and, with her best judgment, mistakenly intensifies the problem by implementing her layers of change. During the following months, Jane gets promoted and John Doe becomes the new replacement; he experiences some problems of his own and further compounds them by incorporating a few new ideas. Soon, you have James Doe and Bruce Doe with their own ideas and solutions to address the issue. Without a systematic process in place, chaos ensues. This bureaucratic dysfunctional system makes no sense to anyone; it's so elaborate and problematic that it requires a full-time engineer to manage the once simple system.

Giving people the freedom to act autonomously and giving them the tools to help facilitate the decision-making process, i.e. the *3 Keys of Execution*, creates stronger tendencies to get the job done. The mistakes that he or she will make in the short-term will be less severe than the long-term consequences of leadership adding unnecessary bureaucratic layers of decision-making, approval, and all other insane control, which kills initiative, commitment and effort.

A thinner policy and procedure manual and less regulatory guidelines can and will substantially improve overall quality and efficiency. We are not suggesting that businesses do away with them, rather streamline them and get out of the way of the people who make the product or deliver the services.

Unclog the Organizational Pipes!

A critical point in creating an execution culture is the flow of and access to information. This one strategic point, allowing the free flow of information within your organization, will give you additional bandwidth to win against your competition.

Most companies make the fatal mistake of hoarding information. If sturdy fences make for bad neighbors then a cache of stored information makes for a slow developing company. Organizations, of course, face external competition regarding information and technology; but, unfortunately, many organizations also create competition from within. This philosophy is better suited for enemies rather than allies.

Many organizational structures drive set patterns for internal competition. This competition creates conflict between teams and consequently, the entire organization. Many will agree that information is power. The compulsive hoarding of information breeds self-interest at the expense of organizational success; information is exploited as a tool "to get ahead," or undermine another department's best interest.

The best way to change the practice of controlling information is by changing behavioral patterns in organizational systems and structures. People who withhold information are by and large a product of their environment. Changing these thinking and behavioral patterns can typically be found in the components of reward systems, promotions, recognition and a host of other adaptive practices.

This is a double-edged sword! Yes, there are various classified pieces of information that are better left with a select few, but there is an unlimited amount of information with non-proprietary and less scale-sensitive information that can spark new ideas, cross pollination and better outcomes. To create a culture of execution, it is PARAMOUNT that everyone can see what everyone is doing. Yes, even the CEO needs to have their actions displayed to the entire organization.

What are you afraid of?

At this point, you have options to address this chronic problem. You must guide new thoughts about the flow of information and how it integrates the business together. The way information is shared is rapidly changing every day and you better get used to it. The technological turbo, supersonic, quantum charged environment is here and it is moving faster than anyone can keep up with! Just from a technological perspective, the number of servers that are being used to power Xbox Live is greater than ALL the computing power that existed in the entire world in 1999. This computing power is indicative of just how fast information is now spreading in the 21st century.

The business pattern of giving employees a backstage pass behind the leadership and information curtain builds innovative capacity and greater advantage to make better and quicker decisions. Only with this level of information can the full extent of problems encountered, and potential opportunities be integrated into the full-scale creative solution. The general principle is, "more information is better than less information."

But this doesn't necessarily imply that individuals will freely share as previously discussed. If the poor syndrome of misaligned systems is incongruent with the expectation to share, you have a responsibility to evolve the differentiating factors to produce the desired behavior. There needs to be a retooling in the organizational framework of systems and processes. This is the correct therapy for the condition, thus why we have created *the Execution in Your Pocket*® system.

It should be noted that people know what is secretly discussed behind the leadership/information curtain. There are always leaks infiltrating in the informal communiqué. Regrettably, the biggest mistake is the advancement of partial, inaccurate information distorting the true reality. But the essence of the assumed idea is cascading throughout the organization. In general, the unraveling of partial communication routinely sends people into panic mode. Fear is notably the purest primate emotion. When people are in fear, the worst of humanity comes out. This fear causes employees to behave irrationally. Transparency of general information is often taken for granted or neglected.

Consider this concept from *Downton Abby*. The family members exchange gossip and private information, blind to the servants carrying out their everyday tasks in the same room. They would then be shocked to discover the staff had already learned of this information! Information is scattered everywhere. It then loses value because, when it's shared, most don't know what to do with it. The staff, in this instance, could not act on information they overheard until they were formally told by the family. The information becomes a perishable commodity. This strikes at the core of the increasing evidence to broadening access to information and building a consistent framework to share. The truth is—information is rarely completely hidden in this, the information age; it is merely diluted over time.

Part of the execution culture framework is determining the value of the information. A few straightforward questions impact the communication channel: Is the information more valuable only in the hands of executive leadership or in the working hands of other employees? Who needs to know? If it must be kept at a certain level, away from the rest of the organization, what will happen when they do find out? Keep reminding yourself, when choosing between simple or complicated, simple is best.

This concept of Shared Information sparks a wide-ranging discussion of silos. Silos are self-made barriers. Arguably, silos are built on weak connection of overinflated egos, misaligned goals, low confidence, fear, and most certainly a failure to communicate.

When we were developing our execution technology system, we knew our system had to force 100% transparency. Without it, the information needed to execute the organization's goal would be severely limited. There is no such thing as a "need-to-know basis" in our technology driven world. *Everyone* in the organization needs to know what everyone is doing. If they don't, the organization's execution pipes will be clogged.

You as the leader need to push information through the entire system and keep it flowing. If the pipeline slows, the general organization will slow down, and you will suffer from information constipation overwhelmingly making the organization sick and toxic. This will kill your business over a period of time!

Driving a Culture of Execution

A deeper investigation reveals that the available evidence, "Organizational DNA" is embedded in the culture to get things done, or, "Professional Will" You drive execution in your organization by ensuring you have a specific call to action and make sure the *3 Keys of Execution* are used. When we see the culture of execution fail, it is often due to the agonizing truth that people lose their GRIT, their will to get the job done! If you truly want to create a culture of execution, you MUST embody *The 3 Keys of Execution,* be the example to those around you. It doesn't matter if you don't have the "title" of a leader.

Everyone knows that not all those with a title are leaders and not all leaders have a title.

As Leaders each of us has the responsibility to craft an environment around us that will provide fertile ground for the culture of execution to grow. Be careful not to diffuse this responsibility! If you want to achieve excellence, start with yourself, and nurture excellence in those around you.

CPSIA information can be obtained
at www.ICGtesting.com
Printed in the USA
LVHW09014220061 9
621757LV00001B/2/P